WATER MONSTERS

Cavendish
Square

New York

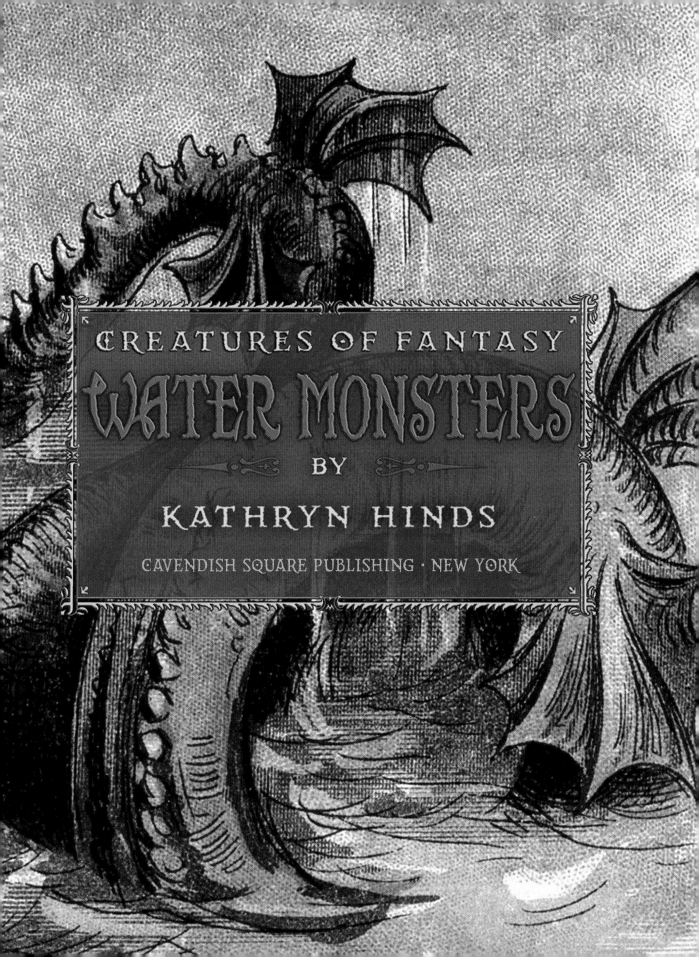

CREATURES OF FANTASY

WATER MONSTERS

BY

KATHRYN HINDS

CAVENDISH SQUARE PUBLISHING · NEW YORK

To Balthazar

LIBRARY OF CONGRESS CATALOGING-IN-PUBLICATION DATA

Hinds, Kathryn, 1962- Water monsters / By Kathryn Hinds. p. cm.—(Creatures of fantasy) Includes bibliographical references and index. Summary: "Explores the mythical and historical backgrounds of water monsters such as the Loch Ness monster, the Vikings' Midgard Serpent, the biblical Leviathan, and the Scandinavian kraken"—Provided by publisher. ISBN 978-0-7614-4926-3 (hardcover)— ISBN 978-1-62712-056-2 (paperback)—978-1-60870-685-3 (ebook) 1. Sea monsters. I. Title. GR910.H57 2012 398.24'54— dc22 2010023598

Editor: Joyce Stanton   Art Director: Anahid Hamparian   Series Designer: Michael Nelson

Photo research by Debbie Needleman. The photographs in this book are used by permission and through the courtesy of: *Front Cover:* © Victor Habbick Visions/Photo Researchers, Inc. *Back Cover:* William M. Rebsamen/Fortean Picture Library. *Page i:* © 2003 Charles Walker/ Topfoto/The Image Works; *pages ii–iii:* © Mary Evans Picture Library/The Image Works; *pages vi, 47:* © The Granger Collection, New York; *page 8:* Bibliotheque Nationale, Paris. © Snark/Art Resource, NY; *page 10:* James Ford Bell Library, University of Minnesota; *page 13:* Ann Ronan Picture Library. © HIP/Art Resource, NY; *page 14:* © The British Library/StockphotoPro; *page 17:* © SuperStock; *page 20:* © The Art Gallery Collection/Alamy; *page 21:* © The Art Archive/SuperStock; *page 22:* Andromeda rescued from the monster by Perseus riding Pegasus, French School (15th century). British Library, London UK. © British Library Board. All Rights Reserved/Bridgeman Art Library; *page 26:* © Musee National de la Renaissance, Ecouen, France/The Bridgeman Art Library/Getty Images; *pages 28, 51:* © Charles Walker/ Topfoto/The Image Works; *page 30:* © Mary Evans/WALT DISNEY PICTURES/Ronald Grant/Everett Collection; *pages 32, 39:* MIT Hart Nautical Collection; *page 33:* © Stephen Frink/CORBIS; *page 34:* © North Wind Picture Archives; *page 37:* © Hulton Archive/Getty Images; *page 41:* © W.M. Horton/CORBIS; *page 43:* © Richard Ellis/Photo Researchers, Inc.; *page 44:* © Fortean/Topham/The Image Works; *pages 46, 54:* © Mary Evans Picture Library/Alamy; *page 50:* © CHARLES R. KNIGHT/NationalGeographicStock.com; *page 52:* © Victor Habbick Visions/Photo Researchers, Inc.; *page 56:* © Lawrence Lawry/Photo Researchers, Inc.

Printed in the United States of America

Front cover: The elusive Loch Ness monster surfaces beneath a full moon.
Back cover: The *mokele-mbembe*, a monster said to live in the rivers of West Africa, imagined as a kind of dinosaur.
Half-title page: A toothy sea monster stirs up the water, creating dangerous conditions for sailors.
Title page: In an illustration from around 1890, a sea monster gazes hungrily at a passing ship.

CONTENTS

On a Swedish map from 1539, a double-spouted monster
is depicted threatening a ship in northern waters.

INTRODUCTION

In the CREATURES OF FANTASY series, we celebrate the deeds of dragons, unicorns, mermaids, water monsters, and more. These fabulous beasts have inhabited the imagination and arts since the beginnings of human history. They have been immortalized in paintings and sculptures, mythology and literature, movies and video games. Today's blockbuster books and films—*The Chronicles of Narnia, Harry Potter, Lord of the Rings, The Hobbit,* and others—have brought new popularity to fans of folklore, myths, and legends. It seems that these creatures of the imagination have always been with us and, in one way or another, always will be.

Belief in the fantastic, in wonders, appears to be a lasting part of the human experience. Even if we no longer believe that dragons and unicorns actually exist, we still like to think about what things might be like if they did. We dream and daydream about them. We make up stories. And as we share those dreams, read and tell those stories, we not only stir our imaginations but also explore some of the deepest hopes and fears of humanity. The power of the dragon, the purity of the unicorn, the wildness of the centaur, the allure of the mermaid—these and more are all part of our human heritage, the legends of our ancestors still alive for us today.

HERE BE
MONSTERS

The vast ocean . . . shows diverse sorts of Fish; and these [are] not only
wonderful for magnitude, . . . they are terrible in shape.

~Olaus Magnus, 1555

IN 1539 A SWEDISH PRIEST KNOWN AS OLAUS Magnus published his Carta Marina, a map of northern Europe. Heavily illustrated with pictures of the people and animals of the region, it shows the sea west of Norway filled with a variety of fantastical creatures. Some can be identified as whales and perhaps walruses, although they are portrayed as fierce and forbidding monsters. There are others even more fanciful: a large, colorful flying fish; a giant scorpion; a sea unicorn; and a creature so big that two tiny-looking sailors have mistaken it for an island and lit a fire on its back.

But this creature is not the worst of the dangers awaiting sailors in these waters. The map also depicts a huge red sea serpent

Opposite: A sixteenth-century French manuscript included this illustration of a navigator so focused on his globe and compass that he does not even notice the strange sea creature approaching his ship.

wrapped around a ship while devouring its crew, a massive orange monster dragging another ship under, and an enormous green beast with a crested back and two jets of water spouting from its head. The beast rises up out of the sea to menace a westward-bound ship and is apparently about to swallow it whole.

Did Olaus Magnus really believe the ocean was full of monsters? Well, in 1555 he followed up his Carta Marina with a book about the northern lands, in which he included a chapter on sea monsters. He wrote, for example, that the fishermen, sailors, and traders on the Norwegian coast

> do all agree on this strange story, that there is a Serpent there which is of a vast magnitude [size], namely

200 foot long, and more—over 20 feet thick; and [typically lives] in Rocks and Caves toward the Sea-coast . . . which will go alone from his holes in a clear night, in Summer, and devour Calves, Lambs, and Hogs, or else he goes into the Sea to feed on Polypus, Locusts, and all sorts of Sea-Crabs. He hath commonly hair hanging from his neck a Cubit* long, and sharp Scales, and is black, and he hath flaming shining eyes. This Snake disquiets the Shippers, and he puts up his head on high like a pillar, and catcheth away men, and he devours them.

In the 1500s, stories about sea serpents like this seemed entirely believable, even to educated people like Olaus Magnus. Immense stretches of ocean were still uncharted. They would remain so for many a year to come, with mapmakers labeling unexplored areas HERE BE MONSTERS. After all, who knew what marvels the waters might hold?

The sea was a vast unknown. Once you left land behind, it could be days, weeks, or months before you came to solid ground again. Meanwhile, you were surrounded by water and sky, and you were at the mercy of the elements. Storms could blow your ship off course, or sink it. The wind could fail, leaving your sails limp and the ship stuck in one spot. Fog could disguise all types of hazards, from icebergs to reefs to rocky coasts. There might be whirlpools. So among all the unknowns, there was one thing you knew for sure: ocean voyages were dangerous.

*A cubit was the length of an adult man's hand and forearm, from the tip of the longest finger to the elbow—on average, 19 to 20 inches.

You also knew that you and your shipmates were not alone at sea; you knew the water was home to untold numbers of creatures. Sometimes you would see marine animals—whales, dolphins, sharks—swimming near the ship. Sometimes you might see creatures that were totally unfamiliar. Some of them might look very strange, even frightening. And when you were in the middle of the ocean, the water was deeper than you could possibly measure. Who knew what might lurk in those depths?

Moreover, as we will read in the following pages, many of the world's legends, ancient histories, and religious writings described wondrous and terrible creatures of the deep. So really, all things considered, it would be surprising if the sailors of earlier times did *not* believe in sea monsters. Even today, there is still much we don't know about the earth's oceans, which cover nearly three-fourths of the planet's surface. Scientists are continually discovering new ocean-dwelling species, many with amazing adaptations to their environments. Looking at some of these creatures, we might wonder if perhaps sea serpents and their kin really do exist. . . .

The Monster That Looks Like an Island

In times past, people in many parts of the world believed there was a sea monster that lured sailors to their death by disguising itself as an island, as depicted on Olaus Magnus's Carta Marina. In Arabic-speaking countries this monster was called the Zaratan. An ancient Greek name for it was the Aspidochelone (which meant "asp-turtle"); an early English poem gave it a similar name, Fastitocalon. In a very old Irish story about the adventures of a sixth-century saint, *The Voyage of Saint Brendan*, the creature was called Jasconius. Much of western Europe knew it as the Cetus—a Latin word that originally meant "sea monster" and also came to mean "whale." (It is the root of our word *cetacean*, which refers to ocean mammals such as whales and porpoises.) Here is a classic description of the Cetus, from a book written around 1210 by a French author named Guillaume le Clerc:

> Just like unto sand is the crest on top of its back. When it rises to the surface in the sea, they who are wont to sail that way quite believe it is an island, but hope deceives them. Because of his great size there they come for safety from the storm that drives them. They think to be in a safe place, they throw out their anchors and gangway, cook their food, light their fire, and to make their ship fast drive great stakes into the sand, which is like land in their opinion. Then they light their fire, I do assure you. When the monster feels the heat of the fire that burns on top of him, then he makes a sudden plunge down into the great deep and drags the ship along with him, and all the crew perish.

Above: Saint Brendan and his followers attending Mass on the back of Jasconius.

זה לויתן "

DWELLERS IN THE DEPTHS

Can you draw out Leviathan with a fishhook,
or press down his tongue with a cord?

~THE BOOK OF JOB

NE OF THE WORLD'S EARLIEST RECORDED sea monster stories was written down roughly 3,500 years ago. Scholars found it in texts discovered along the coast of Syria at Ras Shamra. In ancient times, Ras Shamra was an important port city called Ugarit. The ancient text discovered there is a mythological tale about the god Baal's fight with Yam, the ocean. Yam, described as a seven-headed sea serpent or dragon, was called by many different names: Sea Monster, Crooked Serpent, Close-Coiling One, Tyrant of the Seven Heads, and Lotan.

Although it might not be obvious at first, this last name is closely related to the name of the biblical Leviathan. In the Old Testament book of Job, Leviathan is described this way:

Opposite: Leviathan lies curled in the depths of the sea, from a thirteenth-century Hebrew manuscript.

Out of his mouth go flaming torches; sparks of fire leap forth. Out of his nostrils comes forth smoke, as from a boiling pot and burning rushes. His breath kindles coals, and a flame comes forth from his mouth. In his neck abides strength, and terror dances before him. . . . His heart is hard as a stone, hard as the nether millstone. When he raises himself up the mighty are afraid; at the crashing they are beside themselves. Though the sword reaches him, it does not avail; nor the spear, the dart, or the javelin. . . . He makes the deep boil like a pot. . . . Upon earth there is not his like, a creature without fear. He beholds everything that is high; he is king over all the sons of pride.

Although Psalm 104 praises God for his creation of the sea and "Leviathan which thou didst form to sport in it," other parts of the Bible portray Leviathan as God's enemy. Psalm 74 says, "Thou didst crush the heads of Leviathan, thou didst give him as food for the creatures of the wilderness." According to the book of Isaiah, Leviathan's destruction will come at the end of time: "In that day the Lord with his hard and great and strong sword will punish Leviathan the fleeing serpent, Leviathan the twisting serpent, and he will slay the dragon that is in the sea."

Jewish scholars after biblical times continued to write about Leviathan. Some said that God originally created two leviathans, a male and a female. But then he realized that if they had children, the multiplying offspring might destroy the world, so he killed the female leviathan. Another scholar wrote that Leviathan had a counterpart on land: "And on that day the two monsters

French painter Gustave Doré's 1865 illustration of "the Lord with his hard and great and strong sword" about to slay "Leviathan the twisting serpent."

[were] parted: one, the she-monster Leviathan, to dwell in the abyss of the ocean over the fountains of water, and the other, the male beast named Behemoth, [to dwell] in an invisible desert."

An early rabbi named Johanan wrote, "Once we went in a ship and saw a fish which put his head out of the water. He had horns upon which was written: 'I am one of the meanest [smallest or least important] creatures that inhabit the sea. I am three hundred miles in length, and enter this day into the jaws of the leviathan.'" Rabbi Johanan also wrote that after Judgment Day, God would give the righteous a banquet, at which they would feast on the flesh of Leviathan. In addition, God would use Leviathan's skin to make tents for the most pious people and belts and similar items for others. Afterward he would lay the rest of the hide over the walls of Jerusalem, and so much light would shine from it that the entire world would be illuminated.

Christian writers focused on the description of Leviathan as God's enemy and "king over all the sons of pride." These writers identified Leviathan with Satan, the devil. One of the most famous comparisons between Satan and Leviathan is from *Paradise Lost*, by the seventeenth-century poet John Milton:

> Thus Satan talking to his nearest mate
> With head up-lift above the wave, and eyes
> That sparkling blaz'd, his other parts besides
> Prone on the flood, extended long and large
> Lay floating many a rood*, in bulk as huge
> As . . . that sea-beast

*A rood was an old British measurement equaling between 7 and 8 yards.

Leviathan, which God of all his works
Created hugest that swim th' Ocean stream.

Far away from the lands of the Bible, the Scandinavian people of northern Europe had their own lore about a monstrous sea serpent with a divine enemy. This creature was known as Jormungand, the Midgard Serpent. The thirteenth-century Icelandic writer Snorri Sturluson, who collected together many myths from the time of the Vikings, told how the god Odin "flung the serpent into the deep sea which surrounds the whole world, and it grew so large that it now lies in the middle of the ocean round the earth, biting its own tail."

Although Odin was the leader of the gods, it was his son Thor who became Jormungand's greatest foe. Thor was a much-loved deity, known for his strength and fiery temper. One time he took a giant named Hymir on a fishing trip. As Thor rowed farther and farther out to sea, Hymir began to worry they would have a run-in with the Midgard Serpent. Thor just laughed at Hymir's fears, but he finally stopped rowing and threw out his fishing line, baited with an ox head. As Snorri tells it:

> The Midgard Serpent snapped at the ox-head, but the hook stuck fast in the roof of its mouth and, when it realized that, it jerked away so hard that both Thor's fists knocked against the gunwale. Then Thor grew angry and, exerting [all] his divine strength, dug in his heels so hard that both legs went through the boat and he was digging his heels in on the sea bottom. He drew the serpent up on board, and it must be said that

no one has seen anything to be afraid of who didn't see how Thor fixed the serpent with his eye and how the serpent glared back, belching poison.

At this point Hymir had had enough. He drew his knife and cut Thor's fishing line, allowing the Midgard Serpent to sink back into the sea. In some versions of the story, Thor still managed to kill Jormungand that day. But in others, the creature was destined to remain in the sea until the end of the world. When that time comes, according to Snorri, "The sea will lash against the land because the Midgard Serpent is writhing in giant fury to come ashore." After a great battle, Thor will at last slay Jormungand, "but stagger back only nine paces before he falls down dead, on account of the poison blown on him by the serpent." Everything will be destroyed. Afterward, however, a new earth will rise up out of the sea, and Thor's sons will take his place to protect the world from monsters.

Above: While on his fishing trip with Hymir, Thor prepares to haul the Midgard Serpent aboard and strike it with his hammer. The eighteenth-century Icelandic artist has portrayed the old god as a typical local fisherman of the time.

Jonah's Monstrous Whale

In modern Hebrew, *leviathan* is the word for "whale." And closely related to the Bible's Leviathan was the sea creature that swallowed the reluctant prophet Jonah. As the story goes, God wanted Jonah to go and preach in the city of Nineveh (in what is now Iraq). Jonah was afraid the citizens of Nineveh would be hostile toward him, though, so he got onto a ship sailing in the opposite direction. When a storm came up and threatened to sink the ship, Jonah knew it was because God was angry with him. It looked like all was lost, so he told the sailors to save themselves by throwing him overboard. They did so, and Jonah was promptly swallowed by "a great fish . . . and Jonah was in the belly of the fish three days and three nights."

Many early Christian writers believed this "great fish" was in fact Leviathan. Others thought it was a whale, or a dolphin, or a sea serpent. A sixteenth-century French naturalist believed that it was a great white shark. Whatever it was, it was clearly a monster—and for some, no ordinary monster, but a symbol of death and more. The New Testament book of Matthew says, "For as Jonah was three days and three nights in the belly of the whale, so will [Jesus] be three days and three nights in the heart of the earth." Some early Christians interpreted this to mean that during the days between his death and resurrection, Jesus descended into hell to preach to the suffering souls there. And that made "the belly of the whale," as well as the whale or "great fish" itself, symbols of hell. No wonder so many sailors were terrified of the creatures of the deep!

Above: A twentieth-century Ethiopian folk artist painted this image of Jonah and the "great fish."

HEROIC ENCOUNTERS

At ancient Sikyon, they keep an enormous sea monster skull,
with a statue of the God of Dreams standing behind it.

~Pausanias, second-century Greek historian

THE MYTHS AND LEGENDS OF ANCIENT Greece and Rome were full of fantastic creatures of all kinds. Sea monsters played starring roles in some of the tales, usually as agents of the god of the sea. Known as Poseidon to the Greeks and Neptune to the Romans, he typically sent out his monsters to punish mortals for committing sins against the gods or interfering with divine plans. Only a great hero could defeat such creatures.

A young Greek named Perseus was one such hero, and he'd already had a number of successful adventures before his encounter with the sea monster. It helped that, although his mother was mortal, his father was Zeus, the king of the gods. With his father's blessing, Perseus had received assistance from the god Hermes and the goddess Athena. They gave him the weapons he needed to slay

Opposite:
The ancient Greek hero Perseus as a knight in shining armor, from a manuscript dating to 1410. Aided by the winged horse Pegasus, he arrives just in time to save Andromeda from the terrible sea monster.

Medusa, a snake-haired creature whose single glance could turn a person to stone. After killing her, he carried away her head, which would soon come in very handy.

Perseus was passing through Ethiopia—or in some versions, Joppa (now Jaffa, Israel)—when he encountered a maiden chained to a rock. Her name was Andromeda, and she quickly told him she was there because her mother had boasted about being more beautiful than the goddesses of the sea. Poseidon had sent a sea monster as punishment for this impious pride, and its attacks would only stop if Andromeda were given to it. She had just managed to finish telling Perseus all this when, in the words of the Roman poet Ovid:

> As a galley
> Bears down, with all the sturdy sweating rowers
> Driving it hard, so came the monster, thrusting
> The water on both sides in a long billow. . . .
> When the fangs struck, [Perseus] poised, he sought for openings
> Along the barnacled back, along the sides,
> At tapering fishy tail; the monster's vomit
> Was blood and salty water.

Of course Perseus killed the monster and freed Andromeda, after which the two were married. In some tellings of the story, Perseus won his victory by holding up the head of Medusa; even dead, her eyes still had the power to turn the monster to stone. In other versions, Perseus stabbed or beheaded the creature with his sword. In any case, the first-century Roman writer Pliny the Elder recorded that, about a hundred years before his time, "The skeleton of the monster to which Andromeda in the story was exposed was brought . . .

from the town of Joppa in Judaea and shown at Rome. . . . It was 40 feet long, the height of the ribs exceeding the elephants of India."

No such exhibition was made of the remains of a sea monster slain by another Greek hero, Heracles (Hercules to the Romans), but the story was similar. Disguised as men, Poseidon and Apollo (the god of light) had been hired to build a defensive wall around the city of Troy. The king, named Laomedon, had promised them a generous payment in gold for their work. But when the wall was completed, Laomedon went back on his word and refused to pay them. Ovid tells what happened next:

> "Still, you will pay!" the sea-god roared, and loosed
> His waters over the shore of that stingy country.
> He flooded it to sea, swept off the crops,
> Drowned fields, and this was not enough: the princess,
> Hesione, he ordered, must be given
> As prey to a sea-monster. She was bound
> To the hard cliffs. . . .

Luckily, Heracles came along in time, freed the girl, and killed the monster. Afterward, according to Ovid, Hesione married one of Heracles' friends. The ancient historian Diodorus Siculus, on the other hand, said she went away with Heracles—not just because he had been far kinder to her than her own family had been, "but also because she feared that a Ketos [sea monster] might again appear and she be exposed . . . to the same fate as that from which she had just escaped."

There was no escape from Poseidon's wrath for a later citizen of Troy, during the final days of the Trojan War. After ten years

The Trojans take the great wooden horse into their city, not knowing it conceals their doom.

of besieging the city, the Greek army appeared to give up and go away. They left behind only one man, a soldier named Sinon, and a huge wooden horse. When the Trojans found Sinon, he told them a sob story about how the other Greeks had wanted to sacrifice him to the gods before they left, so he had run away and he now wished to join the Trojans. He also explained that the Greeks had made the horse as an offering to the goddess Athena. The reason for its great size was so that the Trojans would think it was too big to take into their city. If they did take it in, Sinon said, Athena would turn her favor away from the Greeks and toward the Trojans.

The priest Laocoön urged his fellow citizens not to believe Sinon. "I fear the Greeks even when they bear gifts," he declared. Poseidon, still an enemy of Troy, decided to silence him and sent two great serpents out of the sea. They came up onto the land and went straight for Laocoön and his two sons. Quick as a wink, they coiled around the three and crushed them to death.

The Trojans were convinced that the priest had been divinely punished for his doubts. They lost no time in dragging the wooden horse through the city gates. That night Greek soldiers who had been hidden inside the horse crept out and began their final assault on Troy. By morning the city was theirs.

After the long war's end, the Greeks set sail for home, but some had a more difficult journey than others. The most arduous—and exciting—voyage was that of Odysseus. Part of his problem was that he had offended Poseidon, who sent all kinds of storms and foul winds to give him a hard time. Even without Poseidon's anger, there were plenty of hazards at sea for Odysseus. One of the worst was the narrow passage between Scylla and Charybdis. Charybdis was a terrible whirlpool that sucked ships down to the bottom of the sea. Scylla was a monster who had her abode in dangerous rocks just across the water. The *Odyssey,* by the Greek poet Homer, describes Scylla this way:

> Her legs—and there are twelve—
> are like great tentacles,
> unjointed, and upon her serpent necks
> are borne six heads like nightmares of ferocity
> and triple serried rows of fangs and deep
> gullets of black death. Half her length she sways
> her heads in the air, outside her horrid [cave]. . . .
> And no ship's company can claim
> to have passed her without loss and grief; she takes
> from every ship, one man for every gullet.

Indeed, as his ship sailed between Scylla and Charybdis, Odysseus lost six of his men—one swallowed by each of Scylla's heads. Odysseus and the rest got away with their lives only thanks to the protection of Athena. For heroes facing monsters, there was nothing quite so helpful as having one of the gods or goddesses on their side.

4

TENTACLES OF DEATH

"I myself can remember," said Conseil
with the most serious tone of voice in the world,
"having seen a large boat dragged down
by the arms of a squid."

~JULES VERNE, 1869

ONE OF THE MOST FAMOUS SEA MONSTERS in literature is the giant squid in *Twenty Thousand Leagues Under the Sea*, by French novelist Jules Verne. Disney's 1954 film adaptation of the book is likewise a classic, with special effects that brought this menace of the deep to life in a way never seen in the movies before. Here is Verne's description of the giant squid—"a terrible monster worthy of all the legends about such creatures"—shortly before it attacks the submarine *Nautilus*:

The eight arms, or rather legs, coming out of its head—it is this which earned it the name of "ceph-alopod"—were twice as long as its body and were twisting like the hair of a Greek fury. We could clearly

Opposite: A giant squid coils its tentacles around the masts of a French ship and prepares to drag it beneath the waves.

Captain Nemo, played by British actor James Mason, struggles with the giant squid in Disney's 1954 movie *20,000 Leagues Under the Sea.*

make out the 250 suckers lining the inside of its tentacles. . . . The monster's mouth—a horny beak like that of a parakeet—opened and closed vertically. Its tongue, also made of a hornlike substance and armed with several rows of sharp teeth, would come out and shake what seemed like veritable cutlery. What a whim of nature!

Verne may have based his giant squid in part on an 1802 book's description of a French sailing ship being seized off the coast of Africa by a monster with many arms, long enough to reach all the way up the ship's masts. The fierce reputation of the squid went back much further, though—to at least Roman times. Pliny the Elder wrote, "There is not an animal in existence that is more dangerous for its powers of destroying a human being when in the water. Embracing his body, it counteracts his struggles, and draws him under with its feelers and its numerous suckers." Luckily, there was a way to escape, if you could manage it: when "the animal is turned over, it loses all its power; for when it is thrown upon the back, the arms open of themselves."

Pliny called this creature a *polypus*; Verne used a similar French word, *poulpe*. In Scandinavia the word for a squidlike monster was *kraken, krabben,* or *kolkrabbe.* The earliest description seems to come from Olaus Magnus:

> Their Forms are horrible, their Heads square, all set with prickles, and they have sharp and long Horns round about, like a Tree rooted up by the Roots. They are ten or twelve Cubits long, very black, and with huge eyes: . . . the Apple of the Eyes is of one Cubit, and is red and fiery coloured, which in the dark night appears to Fisher-men afar off under Waters, as a burning fire . . . ; one of these Sea-Monsters will drown easily many great ships provided with many strong Mariners.

In the 1750s, Norwegian bishop Erik Pontoppidan called the kraken "incontestably the largest Sea-monster in the world." He wrote that when sighted, it "looks at first like a number of small islands, surrounded with something that floats and fluctuates like sea weeds. . . . At last several bright points or horns appear, which grow thicker and thicker the higher they rise above the surface of the water, and sometimes they stand as high and large as the masts of middle-siz'd vessels."

By the time Pontoppidan was writing, a number of dead giant squid had been found washed up on beaches. One in Iceland in 1639 was described as "a peculiar creature or sea monster." One in Ireland in 1673 was publicly displayed and advertised this way: "A wonderful Fish or Beast . . . which had two heads and Ten

horns, and upon Eight of the said Horns about 800 Buttons . . . and in each of them a set of Teeth, the said Body was bigger than a Horse and was 19 Foot Long Horns and all." In 1790 an even larger specimen washed up in Iceland: it was a total of 39 feet long. Nevertheless, it would take many more decades for the giant squid to be fully acknowledged by science.

As the giant squid became more and more of a reality, the kraken became even more a creature of myth and fantasy. An 1830 poem by Alfred, Lord Tennyson, portrayed it as an ancient creature that lies on the sea bottom awaiting Judgment Day:

Below the thunders of the upper deep,
Far, far beneath the abysmal sea,
His ancient, dreamless, uninvaded sleep
The Kraken sleepeth. . . .
There hath he lain for ages and will lie
Battening upon huge seaworms in his sleep
Until the latter fire shall heat the deep;
Then once by man and angels to be seen,
In roaring he shall rise and on the surface die.

Stranger than Fiction

The giant squid was recognized as a real animal in 1857, when it was given the scientific name *Architeuthis*. For a long time afterward, little was known about it—indeed, it is still largely a mystery to us. But some of the things we have learned indicate that this creature is more amazing than even Jules Verne imagined. *Architeuthis* has not eight but ten arms—two of them are extra-long tentacles that are used when feeding. It also has three hearts and, as in *Twenty Thousand Leagues Under the Sea*, teeth on its tongue.

Verne's giant squid was 25 feet long, which seems like a truly monstrous size. But the average size of *Architeuthis* is probably about twice that, with a weight of around a ton. The largest squid we know of so far, found in New Zealand, was 65 feet long. It can be hard to judge a giant squid's exact size, however, because its tentacles stretch like rubber bands. Its head, or mantle, on the other hand, is tough and nonstretchy, and can have a length of more than 7 feet.

Architeuthis has eyes bigger than hubcaps—the largest eyes of any living creature, in fact. And they are almost as complex as human eyes. Sight seems to be *Architeuthis*'s most finely tuned sense, perhaps because it lives in the darkness of the deep ocean. In 2004 two Japanese scientists filmed a 26-foot-long squid swimming more than half a mile underwater, and this creature almost certainly frequents much greater depths.

Above: A squid's complex eye is adapted to seeing in deep, dark water.

STRANGE SIGHTINGS

*No reasonable person can doubt the fact
of some marine animal of extraordinary dimensions,
and in all probability of the serpent tribe,
having been repeatedly seen by various persons.*
~Captain Arthur de Capell Brooke, 1823

BEGINNING IN THE 1500s AND 1600s, EUROPEAN colonization and trade in the Americas, Africa, and Asia greatly increased ocean traffic, and more ships on the seas meant more sea monster sightings. At the same time, books, newspapers, and other sources of information were becoming more affordable and more widespread than ever before. When a ship's crew or a coastal community spotted a strange ocean creature, it was now possible for huge numbers of people, far and wide, to learn about it. Between the years 1634 and 1964, according to one researcher, there were well over five hundred written reports about sightings of just one kind of marine monster: the sea serpent.

In the 1630s English settlers became perhaps the first Europeans to report seeing sea serpents in North America. Traveler John

Opposite: Surrounded by fog, can a ship's crew be certain they're seeing a sea monster, or could it just be a trick of the uncertain light?

Josselyn recorded that while he was visiting Massachusetts in June 1639, some gentlemen came by his lodging to welcome him and share some of the latest news. They told him about "a sea-serpent or snake, that lay coiled up like a cable upon a rock at Cape Ann: a boat passing by with English aboard, and two Indians, they would have shot the serpent but the Indians dissuaded them, saying, that if [the serpent] were not killed outright, they would be all in danger of their lives." A man named Obidiah Turner also had a sighting in the same area around that time: "a monster . . . which did there come out of the sea and coil himself upon the land."

Early in the eighteenth century, the Danish priest Hans Egede sailed to Greenland to try to convert the Inuit there to Christianity. He wrote a book about his experiences, which included a sighting of "that most dreadful Monster, that showed itself upon the Surface of the Water in the year 1734, off our colony":

> The Monster was of so huge a Size, that coming out of the Water its Head reached as high as the Mast-Head; its Body was as bulky as the Ship, and three or four times as long. It had a long pointed Snout, and spouted like a Whale-Fish; great broad Paws, and the Body seemed covered with shell-work, its skin very rugged and uneven. The under Part of its Body was shaped like an enormous huge Serpent, and when it dived again under Water, it plunged backwards into the Sea and so raised its Tail aloft, which seemed a whole Ship's Length distant from the bulkiest part of its Body.

An 1860 illustration of the sea monster sighted near Greenland by Hans Egede.

In the mid-1700s Bishop Pontoppidan wrote that he had not really believed sea serpents existed "till that suspicion was removed by full and sufficient evidence from creditable and experienced fishermen and sailors in Norway . . . who can testify that they have annually seen them." The yearly appearance of these creatures was said to be in July and August, when calm weather would bring them to the surface. If the wind came up, though, they would plunge back down to their usual habitat at the bottom of the sea.

Pontoppidan found other reliable witnesses, such as Norwegian naval captain Lawrence von Ferry, whose ship had encountered a sea serpent in August 1746. The captain was so convinced of what he had seen that he testified about it to a judge, describing the creature in full:

> The head of this sea-serpent, which it held more than two feet above the water, resembled that of a horse. It was of a greyish color, and the mouth was quite black and very large. It had large black eyes, and a long white mane, which hung down to the sur-

face of the water. Besides the head and neck, we saw seven or eight folds, or coils, of this snake, which were very thick, and as far as we could tell, there was a fathom's distance [6 feet] between each fold.

August 1817 brought one of the most remarkable sea monster appearances of all. What was extraordinary was not only the creature itself but also the number of eyewitnesses. On about half a dozen different days, a couple hundred people or more—some individually and some in groups—saw a strange sight in the waters off Gloucester, Massachusetts. All the observers agreed on what it looked like, although they had trouble reckoning its length, with estimates ranging from 40 to more than 100 feet. Still, no one had any doubt that the creature was, as a Boston news sheet declared, "A Monstrous Sea Serpent: The largest ever seen in America."

There was so much excitement over the Gloucester sea serpent that a scientific society decided to investigate. They collected a number of sworn statements from witnesses. Here is a typical one, from a ship's master named Solomon Allen:

> I have seen a strange marine animal that I believe to be a serpent, in the harbor of said Gloucester. I should judge him to be between eighty and ninety feet in length. . . . His head [was] formed something like the head of a rattlesnake, but nearly as large as the head of a horse. When he moved on the surface of the water, his motion was slow, at times playing about in circles, and sometimes moving nearly straight forward. When he disappeared he sunk apparently directly down.

In 1848 another sighting that attracted widespread attention occurred. Captain Peter M'Quhae of the British navy reported to his superiors that he and several members of his crew had seen something unusual approaching their ship, the *Daedalus*, as it sailed a few hundred miles west of Africa:

The sea serpent in this drawing is said to bear a strong resemblance to the Gloucester monster, described by many eyewitnesses in 1817.

> It was discovered to be an enormous serpent, with head and shoulders kept about four feet constantly above the surface of the sea; and as nearly as we could approximate . . . there was at the very least sixty feet of the animal. . . . It did not, either in approaching the ship or after it had passed our wake, deviate in the slightest degree from its course to the S.W., which it held on at the pace of from twelve to fifteen miles per hour, apparently on some determined purpose. The diameter of the serpent was about fifteen or sixteen inches behind the head, which was, without any doubt, that of a snake. . . . It had no fins, but something like the mane of a horse, or rather a bunch of sea-weed, washed about its back.

Reports of the *Daedalus*'s sea serpent encounter appeared in several London newspapers. The incident was especially notable because of the observer's high rank and his detailed description, and also because it was the first widely known sighting to occur in southern waters. More would follow. And Captain M'Quhae's testimony encouraged several officers from other ships to publish accounts of sightings they'd had in the past, but had been embarrassed to admit to at the time.

Reports of sea serpents continued into the twentieth century. In 1905 a U.S. Army general wrote to the American Museum of Natural History about one he'd seen off the coast of Maine. That same year two English scientists spotted a sea serpent in the waters off Brazil. One of the scientists published a detailed report in the *Proceedings of the Zoological Society of London*:

> I looked and saw a large fin or frill sticking out of the water, dark seaweed-brown in colour, somewhat crinkled on the edge. It was apparently about 6 feet in length. . . . I could see, under the water to the rear of the frill, the shade of a considerable body. I got my field glasses . . . and almost as soon as I had them on the frill, a great head and neck rose out of the water in front of the frill . . . at a distance of not less than 18 inches, probably more. The neck appeared about the thickness of a slight man's body. . . . The head had a turtle-like appearance, as had also the eye. . . . It moved its head from side to side in a peculiar manner; the colour of the head and neck was dark brown above, and whitish below.

In the 1930s people began to report seeing a strange creature in Cadboro Bay, a Pacific inlet in British Columbia, Canada. A newspaper editor decided to call it Cadborosaurus, and people soon nicknamed it Caddy. As of 1993 more than fifty people claimed to have seen Caddy, and sightings have occurred as recently as 2006. Most witnesses have agreed that Caddy looks like a sea serpent with a head shaped like that of a horse or camel. An old whaler who had seen it remembered, "Its long slender body was covered by a furlike material, with the exception of its back, where spiked horny plates overlapped each other. It had skin-covered flippers and a spade-shaped tail."

Another former whaler found a newspaper photo from 1937 that appeared to show a dead Cadborosaurus, and in 1968 he even caught what he thought might be a baby Caddy. (Afraid it would die in captivity, he released it before it could be studied.) As the

A group of men in 1906 pose with a suspiciously stiff-looking sea serpent on a beach in Washington State.

reports mounted, many people came to believe this sea serpent was a creature that had been seen and described by Native Americans and others for hundreds of years, and that its habitat probably extended from Alaska to northern California. Many people are convinced it is no legendary monster but a marine animal previously unknown to science. Two zoologists have even given it a scientific name, *Cadborosaurus willsi*.

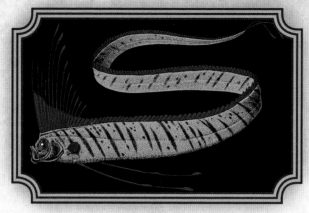

The Amazing Oarfish: A Real-Life Sea Serpent

In 1963 J. R. Norman, a British Museum expert on fish, wrote his solution to at least some sea serpent mysteries: "The monster described as having the head of a horse with a flaming red mane is the Oar-fish or Ribbon-fish, a species which probably grows to more than fifty feet in length, and may sometimes be seen swimming with undulating movements at the surface of the sea." The oarfish itself is a mysterious creature, thought to spend most of its time one to two thousand feet underwater. Oarfish that are seen on the surface are usually dead or dying. Sometimes, though, they have been found washed up on beaches, allowing for close-up observation.

The oarfish has a red fin running all the way down its back, and on its head is a spiny red crest. Its long, slim, silvery body has subtle patterns of spots and short stripes. But it is practically transparent, so it would be difficult to spot one from a distance—which means there are many sea serpent sightings that can't be explained by oarfish. Oarfish are also quite fragile, it seems, and they have no teeth, so they would pose absolutely no threat to humans. But just imagine if you were a sailor and you caught a glimpse of one of these creatures snaking its way alongside your ship, or if you lived near the ocean and saw one lying on the shore. If you didn't know what it was or anything about it, what would you think? Chances are, the first words that would come to your mind would be: SEA SERPENT!

Above: Because of its regal red crest, the giant oarfish is sometimes called the King of Herrings.

MYSTERIOUS WATERS

The great river is very dangerous
when one does not know the difficult places;
it is full of dreadful monsters which would
devour people and canoes altogether.

~Menominee Indians' warning to Jacques Marquette, 1670s

HE OCEANS ARE NOT THE ONLY BODIES OF water where monsters have been thought to live. Rivers, swamps, and lakes may not be vast, but they can still be mysterious—and dangerous. In them, animals and people alike may be sucked down, carried away, drowned, never to be seen again. All but the clearest or shallowest waters can hold secrets, with who-knows-what concealed beneath the surface.

Moreover, water is an unpredictable force. Too much rainfall can make creeks and rivers flood—and perhaps reveal previously hidden terrors. In several countries of northern Europe, there was once a strong belief connecting floods and water monsters. For example, a Norwegian minister reported in 1636 that "in the last flood, a great serpent from the waters came to the sea; he had lived

Opposite: Wherever there's a body of water, monsters may lurk. This sea monster photograph was taken in an Australian lagoon in 1964.

Young John Lambton pulls a strange catch from the river near his home.

up to that point in the Mjös and Branz rivers. From the shores of the latter river, he crossed the fields. People saw him moving like a long ship's mast, overturning all that he met on his path, even trees and huts."

It didn't always take a flood to bring a monster to the surface. A legend from northeastern England tells how, in 1420, wealthy young John Lambton went fishing in the Wear River on Easter Sunday. Instead of a fish, he caught a strange creature with a dragonlike head and a long, slender body. At first Lambton wanted to keep it, but on the way home he decided it was too evil looking, so he threw it into a well. It remained there for several years, growing ever bigger. Then it slithered out and began to attack both animals and people. It was impossible to kill, because even when it was cut in two, it was able to join the pieces of its body back together.

While the serpent was terrorizing the community, John Lambton was away visiting the Holy Land. When he returned home in 1427, he knew it was up to him to put a stop to the monster. He consulted with a local witch, who advised him to attach sharp blades all over his armor and not to fight the creature anywhere except in the middle of the river. Lambton followed these instructions to the letter. When the serpent attacked, it repeatedly tried to coil around him—but every time, the bladed armor sliced off bits of its body. These pieces were carried away by the river current, so the serpent could not put itself back together. That was the end of the water monster known as the Lambton worm.

In Ireland, some lakes were said to be home to monsters called horse-eels. According to a nineteenth-century folklorist, the horse-eel was "seven yards long and as thick as a bull in the body with a mane on its back like a horse." A horse-eel or similar creature that lived in one particular lake was renowned for eating anything that dared enter the water. There is a story about an Englishman who wanted to go swimming in that lake. The local people had warned him about the monster, though, so "he threw his dog in first and it vanished in a swirl."

When English and French explorers arrived in North America, they routinely received warnings about water monsters from the Indians. For instance, the Abenakis cautioned the French of early-1600s Quebec not to make loud noises or fire their guns when traveling by water. If they did, they might disturb the Meskag-kwedemos ("swamp creature"), a ferocious monster that was strongly attracted to noise and violence. The Abenakis sometimes turned this to their advantage during wartime, when they would "take hold of the enemy's canoes to capsize them . . . so the Meskag-kwedemos will rise from the depths to eat them."

This is just one of the numerous water monsters that appear in traditional Native American lore. They are of many types. The Ojibwas, for instance, have stories about a giant sturgeon that lives in Lake Superior; they say this fish is so large it can "hold an entire . . . village in its mouth." Another Ojibwa water monster is called Mishipizhiw, or the Great Lynx, imagined as a huge water-dwelling cat with a sharp-ridged back. A seventeenth-century French trapper recorded that Mishipizhiw "stays at a very

An Ojibwa rock painting on the northern shore of Lake Superior shows the water monster Mishipizhiw.

deep level, and has a long tail which raises great winds when it moves to go to drink; but if it wags its tail energetically it brings about violent tempests."

The Cherokees tell of a giant leech, as big as a house. Red with white stripes, it makes its home where two rivers flow together near Murphy, North Carolina. One day some men spotted it lying on a rock ledge:

> It rolled up into a ball and again stretched out at full length, and at last crawled down the rock and was out of sight in the deep water. The water began to boil and foam, and a great column of white spray was thrown high in the air and came down like a waterspout upon the very spot where the men had been standing, and would have swept them all into the water but that they saw it in time and ran from the place. More than one person was carried down in this way, and their friends would find the body afterwards lying upon the bank.

Iroquois legend tells of a horned serpent that lived in a cavern at the head of Lake Ontario. The Iroquois hero Gun-No-Da-Ya tried to defeat the serpent, but his arrows were lost in the froth churned up by its tail. The serpent must have been impressed by his efforts, though, because it made him an offer: "I am your friend and I will teach you how to harpoon fish at night. I will reveal all of the secrets of the waters. Come with me. I will guide you to my dwelling in the rocks, at the bottom, where the sun never shines." When Gun-No-Da-Ya refused, the serpent swallowed him and took him

to the depths anyway. Eventually he was rescued by Thunder, the only being strong enough to overcome the serpent.

The enmity between thunder beings and water monsters is a theme in many Native American stories. In a Sioux myth, for example, the first age of the world was dominated by reptiles ruled by Unktehi, the water monster. There were no humans around yet, but the reptiles found plenty of other creatures to eat. The reptiles devoured so many living things, both on land and in the water, that they threw nature out of balance. Finally the Thunder Birds blasted Unktehi and the other monstrous reptiles with lightning, turning them to stone.

Unktehi was apparently not just a single powerful ancient being but also a specific type of water monster. Its shape changed, though, along with the Sioux's environment. The first time a European heard and wrote down traditions about Unktehi was around 1680, in Dakota Sioux lands in Minnesota. The Dakotas described Unktehi as a huge buffalo that lived under a waterfall. In the early 1800s geologist Henry Rowe Schoolcraft, visiting Minnesota, also heard that the monster was cattlelike, and "its horns could extend to the skies and its body could swell to cause floods or whirlpools." By this time, however, some Sioux bands—the Lakota and Oglala— had moved westward, to the northern Great Plains. There, Unktehi came to be thought of as "a giant scaly snake with feet." Like its king-size buffalo form, the serpent had horns.

The idea of horned water monsters probably came from the sight of mammoth or mastodon skeletons eroding out of swamps and riverbanks—the prehistoric animals' tusks would have been explained as the creatures' horns. In fact, in 1834 a missionary recorded that the Dakotas of Minnesota showed him Unktehi bones

The mastodon, an early relative of the elephant, died out in North America about 11,000 years ago.

that were the fossilized remains of woolly mammoths. Since the "bones were found in low and wet places, they concluded that their dwelling was in water." Schoolcraft similarly reported, "The fossil bones of the Mastodon . . . they [the Dakotas] confidently believe to be the bones" of Unktehi.

Farther west, in the Great Plains region, fossils of mammoths and mastodons are replaced by those of another long-extinct animal, the mosasaur. This was a large reptilian creature that lived in the prehistoric ocean. Mosasaur skeletons look like they belonged to gigantic snakes, and their skulls are long, narrow, and toothy—much like the heads of water monsters portrayed in some Native American art.

A Lakota holy man named Lame Deer told of an experience he had with a mosasaur skeleton laid bare by erosion. In the early 1900s he was caught in a sudden thunderstorm in the Badlands of South Dakota. Afraid of being swept away by a flash flood, he climbed to a high ridge, crawled along it, and clung there all night long. When morning came, "I saw that I was straddling a long row of petrified bones, the biggest I had ever seen. I had been moving along the spine of the Great Unktehi." Lame Deer explained, "What you people call fossils, these too are used by us. Deep in the Badlands we find the bones of the water monster, which lived long before human beings appeared."

Fearsome in Many Forms

Water monsters are not limited to snakelike or lizardlike creatures but can come in a variety of shapes. Some old Welsh stories feature a flood-causing water monster called the *afanc* or *addanc*, often described as a kind of ferocious giant beaver. The Aboriginal people of Australia tell of the *bunyip*, a huge, carnivorous, hairy creature with claws and tusks that lives in swamps, rivers, and similar places. If its young are threatened, it will cause floods, and anyone touched by the floodwaters will be turned into a black swan.

A West African water monster called the *mokele-mbembe*, or "river stopper," is said to be as large as an elephant, with one great tooth or horn, a long neck, and a tail similar to a snake's or crocodile's. It does not like humans and overturns their boats whenever it gets a chance. The *makara* of Southeast Asia has the tail and body of a fish but the head of a crocodile, although sometimes it is depicted as part crocodile and part bird, or even as a giant crab. A more or less friendly monster, it is ridden on by the Hindu sky god Varuna and is also connected to the goddess of the Ganges River in India.

In Japanese folklore there is a creature called a *kappa* that lives in ponds and rivers. With its froglike legs, monkey face, and tortoise body, it may look friendly, but it has the terrifying habit of kidnapping and eating children. It is, however, extremely polite and can often be tricked by good manners. If you meet a kappa beside the water, bow low to it, and it will return the bow. When it does, it will spill the water pooled in the top of its head, which is the only thing that gives it power to move about on land. If it finds you in the water, though, you're out of luck.

Above: The Hindu god Krishna wrestles with a crocodile-like *makara*.

NESSIE AND HER KIN

There are, it seems, mightier creatures,
and the lake may hide what neither net nor line can take.
~WILLIAM BUTLER YEATS, 1902

W E HAVE SEEN HOW AT LEAST SOME WATER
monster lore seems to have been inspired by the fossils of prehistoric animals. But could some other water
monsters be explained as "living fossils"—the modern-day descend-
ants of creatures from the time of the dinosaurs? Many people
have thought so. In 1893, for example, British biologist Thomas
Henry Huxley wrote that there was no reason he knew of "why
snake-bodied reptiles, from fifty feet long and upwards, should not
disport themselves in our seas as they did in those of the cretaceous epoch."*

The best-known of these possibly "cretaceous" reptiles—
indeed, the most famous of all water monsters—is the monster

*The Cretaceous period ended 65 million years ago.

Opposite:
"Nessie," the Loch
Ness monster, is
thought by some to
belong to a species
that has survived
from the age of
the dinosaurs.

of Loch Ness, a deep, cold lake in the Highlands of Scotland. The earliest record of this creature comes from a seventh-century biography of Saint Columba, who had lived about a hundred years earlier. On a journey, Columba needed to cross the Ness River, which flows out of the northern end of the loch. There was a boat on the other side, and a man named Lugne volunteered to swim across and bring it back. The monster, however, was lurking in the depths.

"Feeling the water above disturbed by Lugne's swimming, it suddenly swam up to the surface, and with gaping mouth and with great roaring rushed towards the man." Everyone on the shore was paralyzed by terror, except Saint Columba:

Saint Columba, near the end of his adventure-filled and holy life, says farewell to his beloved horse.

The blessed man, who was watching, raised his holy hand and drew the saving sign of the cross in the empty air; and then, invoking the name of God, he commanded the savage beast, and said: "You will go no further. Do not touch the man; turn backward speedily." Then, hearing the command of the saint, the beast, as if pulled back with ropes, fled terrified in swift retreat.

More than a thousand years passed before anyone again reported seeing the Loch Ness monster. There were occasional sightings in the 1800s, and then in May 1933 a Scottish newspaper ran a piece titled "Strange Spectacle in Loch Ness." According to the article, a couple driving along the shore noticed a disturbance in the water. They stopped their car and saw a creature "rolling and plunging for fully a minute, its body resembling that of a whale, and the water cascading and churning like a simmering cauldron." As it turned out, the article was greatly exaggerated—the couple later said that what they had seen actually appeared to be "two ducks fighting."

Nevertheless, people were now on the lookout for a monster. August 1933 brought another newspaper report, this time of a sighting on land. A man said that while driving beside the loch, he had seen something like "a pre-historic animal" cross the road in front of him. He described it as being 6 to 8 feet in length, with a long neck that rippled as it walked. As another person commented to the newspaper, what the man observed was quite likely a large otter.

Still, public enthusiasm for the Loch Ness monster—nick-named Nessie—continued to grow. Definite proof of the creature's existence seemed to come in April 1934, when a London doctor named Robert Wilson said he'd taken a photo of Nessie. The picture became famous, and inspired even more people to visit Loch Ness in hopes of seeing the monster. A 1962 eyewitness gave a typical description: "It was thick in the middle and tapered at the extremities. It was sort of blackish-grey in colour. . . . Its size . . . was between 40 and 45 feet long. No details were visible. . . . It was simply an elongated shape moving purposefully to and fro at the edge of the deep water."

Beginning in the 1960s, a number of expeditions were launched to systematically study the loch and find certain evidence of Nessie's existence. The National Geographic Society made one of the most

A plesiosaur fossil, more than 200 million years old, excavated in China. Plesiosaurs could be as much as 40 feet long. If you didn't know about dinosaurs and other prehistoric reptiles, what would you think if you found a fossil like this?

thorough examinations of the lake in 1976, using the latest technology. Despite sonar scans, the positioning of sophisticated underwater cameras, and the work of an assortment of divers, photographers, and marine scientists, the searchers found no sign of any monster.

Other studies of Loch Ness have also come up empty-handed. Moreover, in the mid-1990s it was revealed that Dr. Wilson's 1934 photograph had been faked. The "monster" was actually a head and neck molded from wood putty and attached to a toy submarine. But in spite of hoaxes and lack of scientific proof, Nessie has many believers, and sightings have continued into the twenty-first century. Some people think the Loch Ness monster is a giant eel of some kind, while others think it is a prehistoric animal such as a plesiosaur (a long-necked aquatic reptile). Still others maintain that Nessie is an animal not yet known to science.

Whatever the Loch Ness monster may be, it apparently is not alone: hundreds of lakes all over the world are said to be home to similar creatures. Some have become rather famous. Like Nessie, they have friendly nicknames and draw monster hunters and crowds of tourists. Among them are Morag of Loch Morar (in Scotland), Champ of Lake Champlain (along the New York-Vermont border), Memphre of Lake Memphremagog (spanning the Vermont-Quebec border), Cressie of Lake Crescent (in Newfoundland), Ogopogo of Lake Okanagan (in British Columbia), and Kingstie of Lake Ontario (its name comes from a number of sightings that have occurred near the Canadian city of Kingston).

Many people think these lake monsters are the same kind of creatures identified as sea serpents, or closely related to them. If they are modern plesiosaurs or something like that, their ancestors may have been trapped in the lakes when the seas receded millions of years ago. Or they may be able to travel between their lakes and the ocean by way of rivers or even underground tunnels. Or perhaps they are like the Lindorm, a serpent described in Scandinavian folklore. It is believed to begin life as a little snake, living in ponds and other small bodies of water. As it grows, it migrates to bigger and bigger lakes, crawling over land if necessary. When it is finally too big for any lake to hold it, it moves out to the ocean, where it becomes a sea serpent.

Do lake monsters and sea serpents exist? Well, the answer partly depends on how you define those terms. There certainly are serpentlike creatures that live in the sea—eels, oarfish, and so on. And *monster* has often been used as a description of any large and unfamiliar creature. Many marine animals now acknowledged by science were once called "monsters," including giant squids, walruses, and many kinds of sharks and whales. And as we mentioned in chapter 1, new discoveries are being made all the time, continually increasing our knowledge of the world around us.

So perhaps the last word here should go to steamship commander Sir Arthur Rostron. In 1933 he told a British newspaper about his sighting of "an amazing sea monster" off the coast of Ireland in 1907. He gave a detailed description of the creature, concluding, "There are people who laugh and sneer when they hear talk of the 'sea serpent' but I tell you, no one in this world knows what strange creatures live in the depths of the ocean."

Glossary

Aboriginal Refers to the original people of Australia.

carnivorous Meat-eating.

cephalopod Ancient Greek for "head-foot," this is now the scientific name for the group of tentacled marine animals that includes squids and octopuses.

deity A goddess or god.

folklorist Someone who studies a people's traditional stories, songs, beliefs, and practices.

Inuit The name that most people commonly known as Eskimos prefer to use for themselves.

myth A traditional story about divine and semidivine beings.

mythology A body or collection of myths, such as the myths of a particular people.

naturalist Someone who studies plants, animals, or other aspects of nature.

undulating Wavelike, rolling, coiling, twisting—a snakelike movement.

To Learn More about Water Monsters

Books

Godfrey, Linda S. *Lake and Sea Monsters.* New York: Chelsea House, 2008.

Krensky, Stephen. *Creatures from the Deep.* Minneapolis, MN: Lerner Publications, 2008.

Miller, Karen. *Monsters and Water Beasts: Creatures of Fact or Fiction?* New York: Henry Holt, 2007.

Shovlin, Paul, ed. *Lake Monsters: Fact or Fiction?* Detroit, MI: Greenhaven Press, 2005.

Websites

American Museum of Natural History. *Mythic Creatures.*
www.amnh.org/exhibitions/past-exhibitions/mythic-creatures

British Columbia Scientific Cryptology Club. *Cadborosaurus.*
www.bcscc.ca/cadborosaurus.htm

Krystek, Lee. *The Museum of UnNatural Mystery: Cryptozoology.*
www.unmuseum.org/lostw.htm

Morell, Virginia. "Sea Monsters." *National Geographic.*
http://ngm.nationalgeographic.com/2005/12/sea-monsters/morell-text

Scott, Michon. *Strange Science: Sea Monsters.*
www.strangescience.net/stsea2.htm

WGBH Educational Foundation. *NOVA Online: The Beast of Loch Ness.*
www.pbs.org/wgbh/nova/lochness

SELECTED BIBLIOGRAPHY

Allan, Tony. *The Mythic Bestiary: The Illustrated Guide to the World's Most Fantastical Creatures.* London: Duncan Baird, 2008.

Beck, Horace. *Folklore and the Sea.* Edison, NJ: Castle Books, 1999.

Borges, Jorge Luis. *The Book of Imaginary Beings.* New York: Penguin Books, 2005.

Delacampagne, Ariane, and Christian Delacampagne. *Here Be Dragons: A Fantastic Bestiary.* Princeton, NJ: Princeton University Press, 2003.

Ellis, Richard. *Monsters of the Sea.* New York: Alfred A. Knopf, 1994.

Gould, Charles. *Dragons, Unicorns, and Sea Serpents: A Classic Study of the Evidence for Their Existence.* 1886. Reprint, Mineola, NY: Dover, 2002.

Harrison, Paul. *Sea Serpents and Lake Monsters of the British Isles.* London: Robert Hale, 2001.

Mayor, Adrienne. *The First Fossil Hunters: Paleontology in Greek and Roman Times.* Princeton, NJ: Princeton University Press, 2000.

———. *Fossil Legends of the First Americans.* Princeton, NJ: Princeton University Press, 2005.

Meurger, Michel, and Claude Gagnon. *Lake Monster Traditions: A Cross-Cultural Analysis.* London: Fortean Tomes, 1988.

Nigg, Joseph. *The Book of Fabulous Beasts: A Treasury of Writings from Ancient Times to the Present.* New York: Oxford University Press, 1999.

Radford, Benjamin, and Joe Nickell. *Lake Monster Mysteries: Investigating the World's Most Elusive Creatures.* Lexington: University Press of Kentucky, 2006.

Rose, Carol. *Giants, Monsters, and Dragons: An Encyclopedia of Folklore, Legend, and Myth.* New York: W. W. Norton, 2000.

Stonehouse, Frederick. *Haunted Lakes: Great Lakes Ghost Stories, Superstitions and Sea Serpents.* Duluth, MN: Lake Superior Port Cities, 1997.

NOTES ON QUOTATIONS

Chapter 1

p. 9   "The vast ocean . . . shows diverse": Nigg, *The Book of Fabulous Beasts*, p. 262.

p. 10   "do all agree on this": Ibid., pp. 264-265.

p. 13   "Just like unto sand": Delacampagne, *Here Be Dragons*, p. 60.

Chapter 2

p. 15   "Can you draw out Leviathan": Job 41:1 (Revised Standard Version).

p. 16   "Out of his mouth": Job 41:19-34 (RSV).

p. 16   "Leviathan which thou didst form": Psalms 104:26 (RSV).

p. 16   "Thou didst crush the heads": Psalms 74:14 (RSV).

p. 16   "In that day the Lord": Isaiah 27:1 (RSV).

p. 16 "And on that day": Allan, *The Mythic Bestiary*, p. 202.

p. 18 "Once we went in a ship": Emil G. Hirsch and others, "Leviathan and Behemoth," *The Jewish Encyclopedia*, www.jewishencyclopedia.com

p. 18 "Thus Satan talking": Nigg, *The Book of Fabulous Beasts*, p. 294.

p. 19 "flung the serpent into the deep": Snorri Sturluson, *The Prose Edda: Tales from Norse Mythology*, translated by Jean I. Young (Berkeley: University of California Press, 1954), p. 56.

p. 19 "The Midgard Serpent snapped": Ibid., p. 80.

p. 20 "The sea will lash": Ibid., pp. 86-87.

p. 20 "but stagger back": Ibid., p. 88.

p. 21 "a great fish": Jonah 1:17 (RSV).

p. 21 "For as Jonah": Matthew 12:40 (RSV).

Chapter 3

p. 23 "At ancient Sikyon": Mayor, *The First Fossil Hunters*, p. 228.

p. 24 "As a galley": Ovid, *Metamorphoses*, translated by Rolfe Humphries (Bloomington: Indiana University Press, 1955), p. 104.

p. 24 "The skeleton of the monster": Mayor, *The First Fossil Hunters*, p. 274.

p. 25 "Still, you will pay": Ovid, *Metamorphoses*, translated by Rolfe Humphries (Bloomington: Indiana University Press, 1955), pp. 265-266.

p. 25 "but also because she feared": Diodorus Siculus, *The Library of History*, quoted in Aaron J. Atsma, "Ketos Troias," *The Theoi Project: Guide to Greek Mythology*, www.theoi.com/Ther/KetosTroias.html

p. 26 "I fear the Greeks": Edith Hamilton, *Mythology* (Boston: Little, Brown, 1942), p. 285.

p. 27 "Her legs—and there are twelve": Ellis, *Monsters of the Sea*, p. 123.

Chapter 4

p. 29 "I myself can remember": Ellis, *Monsters of the Sea*, p. 118.

p. 29 "a terrible monster" and "The eight arms": Ibid., p. 115.

p. 30 "There is not an animal" and "the animal is turned over": Pliny the Elder, *The Natural History*, bk. 9, chap. 48, translated by John Bostock, www.perseus.tufts.edu

p. 31 "Their Forms are horrible": Nigg, *The Book of Fabulous Beasts*, p. 264.

p. 31 "incontestably the largest" and "looks at first": Ellis, *Monsters of the Sea*, p. 125.

p. 31 "a peculiar creature" and "A wonderful Fish": Ibid., p. 126.

p. 32 "Below the thunders": Borges, *The Book of Imaginary Beings*, pp. 118-119.

Chapter 5

p. 35 "No reasonable person can doubt": Gould, *Dragons, Unicorns, and Sea Serpents*, p. 275.

p. 36 "a sea-serpent or snake": John Josselyn, *An Account of Two Voyages to New-England, Made during the Years 1638, 1663*, Wisconsin Historical Society, *American Journeys*, http://content.wisconsinhistory.org/u?/aj,8948 (spelling modernized).

p. 36 "a monster . . . which did": Ellis, *Monsters of the Sea*, p. 49.

p. 36 "that most dreadful Monster" and "The Monster was": Ibid., p. 44.

p. 37 "till that suspicion": Gould, *Dragons, Unicorns, and Sea Serpents*, pp. 264-265.

p. 37 "The head of this sea-serpent:" Ellis, *Monsters of the Sea*, p. 45.

p. 38 "A Monstrous Sea Serpent": Ibid., p. 49.

p. 38 "I have seen a strange": Beck, *Folklore and the Sea*, p. 266.

p. 39 "It was discovered to be": Gould, *Dragons, Unicorns, and Sea Serpents*, p. 293.

p. 40 "I looked and saw": Ellis, *Monsters of the Sea*, p. 64.

p. 41 "Its long slender body": Ibid., p. 72.

p. 43 "The monster described": Ibid., p. 43.

Chapter 6

p. 45 "The great river": Meurger and Gagnon, *Lake Monster Traditions*, pp. 189-190.

p. 45 "in the last flood": Ibid., p. 149.

p. 47 "seven yards long" and "he threw his dog": Harrison, *Sea Serpents and Lake Monsters of the British Isles*, p. 201.

p. 47 "take hold of the enemy's": Mayor, *Fossil Legends of the First Americans*, p. 12.

p. 47 "hold an entire": Stonehouse, *Haunted Lakes*, p. 167.

p. 47 "stays at a very deep": Meurger and Gagnon, *Lake Monster Traditions*, p. 167.

p. 48 "It rolled up": James Mooney, *James Mooney's History, Myths, and Sacred Formulas of the Cherokees* (Asheville, NC: Historical Images, 1992), pp. 329-330.

p. 48 "I am your friend": Meurger and Gagnon, *Lake Monster Traditions*, p. 177.

p. 49 "its horns could extend": Mayor, *Fossil Legends of the First Americans*, p. 235.

p. 49 "a giant scaly snake": Ibid., p. 237.

p. 50 "bones were found": Ibid., p. 234.

p. 50 "The fossil bones": Ibid., p. 235.

p. 50 "I saw that I was straddling": Ibid., p. 223.

p. 50 "What you people call fossils": Ibid., p. 220.

Chapter 7

p. 53 "There are, it seems": Meurger and Gagnon, *Lake Monster Traditions*, p. 9.

p. 53 "why snake-bodied reptiles": Harrison, *Sea Serpents and Lake Monsters of the British Isles*, p. 20.

p. 54 "Feeling the water above": Nigg, *The Book of Fabulous Beasts*, p. 148.

p. 54 "The blessed man": Ibid.

p. 55 "Strange Spectacle in Loch Ness": Radford and Nickell, *Lake Monster Mysteries*, p. 11.

p. 55 "rolling and plunging" and "two ducks fighting": Harrison, *Sea Serpents and Lake Monsters of the British Isles*, p. 181.

p. 55 "a pre-historic animal": Radford and Nickell, *Lake Monster Mysteries*, p. 13.

p. 55 "It was thick": Ellis, *Monsters of the Sea*, p. 25.

p. 57 "an amazing sea monster": Harrison, *Sea Serpents and Lake Monsters of the British Isles*, p. 202.

p. 57 "There are people who laugh": Ibid., p. 203.

Index

ABOUT THE AUTHOR

KATHRYN HINDS grew up near Rochester, New York. She studied music and writing at Barnard College, and went on to do graduate work in comparative literature and medieval studies at the City University of New York. She has written more than forty books for young people, including *Everyday Life in the Roman Empire*, *Everyday Life in the Renaissance*, *Everyday Life in Medieval Europe*, and the books in the series BARBARIANS, LIFE IN THE MEDIEVAL MUSLIM WORLD, LIFE IN ELIZABETHAN ENGLAND, and LIFE IN ANCIENT EGYPT. Kathryn lives in the north Georgia mountains with her husband, their son, and two cats. When she is not reading or writing, she enjoys dancing, gardening, knitting, and taking walks in the woods. Visit Kathryn online at www.kathrynhinds.com